/ a rope tossed / to the drowning . . . we rise like / doves from the ashes / of our lives." He counsels us: " . . . I trust / the inward light of poetry / verse radiates the heat of the sun."

So, warm yourself in the wisdom of Arlice W. Davenport. In "The Unprotected Shore," we find him still marching on: "No rearview mirror / of regret . . . / No footprints / behind me. / I keep walking."

And treat yourself to a look at the world through ever-new eyes of an aging poet: "a stand of oaks sambas / in the breeze / they whisper / the important thing is *to move*" ("Who Paints the Breeze"); "The light of my poems lengthens near dusk" ("Light Among the Ruins"); "nature flings its graces in our path / they glimmer like mica in uncut stones" ("Wilderness").

I did so and found a bevy of poems, words, and phrases that are now heartfelt pieces of advice I will carry with me and utter to myself, as I go. Among them are these:

> my father's legacy dies within me
> I carry his book of rules
> like a coffin with no lid
> a long gray wooden rectangle
> full of admonition and hope
> phrases spill out like stones
> carved in unknown hieroglyphs
> (from "Stones")

> love never dies
> it races like atrial fibrillation
> across our hollow chests
> soars over

every limit to desire
rips away each sluggish
shred of doubt
(from "Love Never Dies")

drenched in the *élan vital*
I draw a map to the treasure
of our marriage unwilling
to settle for memory's bright mirage
tonight the moon will burnish
my dreams with beams of you
(from "I Widen the Map's X")

I suspect that you will also find thoughts in this book that will resonate within you, words that make you sing, chant, or bellow to yourself. Davenport says, "my hands work as well / as a chalice I will sip / the water turned hope." In *Traces of the Holy*, these waters run deep and wide, a glittering draught. I urge you to take a sip—begin to quench your thirst.

—Roy Beckemeyer, author of *The Currency of His Light*

AN APPRECIATION OF ARLICE W. DAVENPORT'S *TRACES OF THE HOLY*

These days, with divisiveness and anger, insult and derision making discourse, compromise, standing for a moment in the "other's" shoes, difficult or seemingly impossible, the thoughtful among us often turn to prayer, or to poetry, or to philosophy, or to all three in a search for a path forward, seeking out words of knowledge, insight, understanding, words to verify that the world has made its way through darker times than even these and found the way back to light once again, words that might be signposts along that way.

In his fifth book of poetry, *Traces of the Holy*, Arlice W. Davenport once again puts forward his thoughts and ruminations about life as poems, this time set against his lifelong readings and study in philosophy, literature and theology; poems that sometimes sing, sometimes bellow, that allude to, that delineate nuggets of truth or wisdom or hints at how to find them. This is a book to approach with a highlighter, a pencil or pen, a notebook or a recorder. A book to be read aloud, but it is also a book to browse, a book offering up glints, gems, koans, mantras, those intuitive insights that make some poetry so rewarding to read.

In his opening poem, "Hymn for Hölderlin by Way of an Introduction," Davenport states his lofty goal for this collection: ". . . calm recollection by those / who are most daring summons / the strength of surpassing . . . / And with the inward / force of poetry / all is preserved." Lofty aim, and one that he then sets out to achieve.

Each of the four chapters of this remarkable assemblage opens with a quote from the 19th-century German poet Friedrich Hölderlin. In the first quote is the charge Davenport takes up in his "Hymn for Hölderlin:" To be a poet in a destitute time means: *to attend*, openly, *to the traces of the Holy.* In the following chapters he proceeds to find such traces—First "In the World," then "Within the Self," "At the Heights," and finally, "For the Dying." Of course, those also comprise four ways of looking at ourselves: public, private, aspirational, but always finite, hopefully finding in the end a timeless self, an abiding soul: "spirit is universal," Davenport says, "it warms us /each night in this fragile sack of skin." He joins other poets "who pin couplets onto sestinas / stitch similes into stanzas / who climb the dark rungs of Being / as imagery morphs into metaphor," offering his take from the viewpoint of a life lived long and well, thoughtfully and introspectively ("Other Worlds").

There is hope running rampant through these poems; they recognize the new-moon-midnight-blackness but inevitably turn toward the light of the multitudes of stars and galaxies that we as a whole can bring to bear on the world; Davenport says it this way: "my hand punctures a cloud / tickles the glimmer of stars / glitter dapples my thumb / burns like wildfire up my arm" ("Ascent").

Listen to this: "somewhere you'll find a beatitude // spirit is all we have / that and the freedom to weep / over the furthest reaches of tragedy . . . let us celebrate the freedom . . . to climb the wall of meaning before / kicking away our ladder to the sun" ("Other Worlds").

In a poem titled "The Labyrinth of Love," Davenport shows us how "the sun paints the wall / in speckled shadows / darkness and light tie / themselves into knots

APPRECIATION II

The first thing you should know about Arlice W. Davenport is that he is a philosopher in the Continental traditions of existentialism and phenomenology. He has been shaped by such thinkers as Jean-Paul Sartre, Edmund Husserl, Albert Camus, and Søren Kierkegaard, the nineteenth-century Dane often called the father of existentialism. What is common to all of them is a sure focus on consciousness, Being, and the human self. And if you have been pondering issues of existential meaning, Davenport's fifth collection of poems, *Traces of the Holy*, will help kick-start your journey to the inward depths of your soul.

The best thing to do, I think, to get a feel for the power of this book is to take it into nature. There, with your self fully immersed in the world, you will become aware of the *now*, the only time you have at your disposal, the moments that Davenport so often invokes.

Another thing you will learn with *Traces of the Holy* in hand is that we all are made for love, both *eros* and *agape*. And this book unobtrusively leads you to the Source of those loves. What I discovered is that each type of love is not only shaped by words, but also resonates as the still, small voice within.

* * *

As a poet, Davenport reflects not only on his position in life, but also on the position of humanity in general, beyond the realm of our individual actions. He is obsessed with poetry.

In his poems, he directly or indirectly alludes to other poets and their works. His dialogues with them are no longer his own: We participate in them as we read.

On the one hand, the poet shows us his vulnerability, anxieties, and fears, and on the other, he reveals his haven in the myriad worlds of poetry.

Traces of the Holy consists of four sections, as do all of Davenport's books. The first, "Traces of the Holy: in the World," offers a set of poems in which he contemplates the tension between his dreams and his actions in the world and society. To catch the flavor of this section, I recommend you focus on the poem, "Such Stuff as Dreams Are Made On."

In the second section, "Traces of the Holy: within the Self," the author focuses on himself and his inner world in relation to a higher reality. For some, it may be God. For others, it may be the universe as a whole. In the poem, "The Way to the Sky," he expresses the view that it is necessary to make a sacrifice, to deny oneself for the sake of the greater good.

In the third division, "Traces of the Holy: at the Heights," the reader can observe Davenport's thoughts about life and death, about what kind of trace we leave behind. "Love Never Dies" is a fine example of such a lasting trace:

> love never dies
> its body is the Other
> whom we can never reach
> we cradle it in our mind
> caress its imaginary flesh
> then preserve it as *caritas*
> fixing it forever
> above the stars[.]

In "Traces of the Holy: for the Dying," the last section of the book, Davenport comes to terms with his mortality, accepting its vulnerability, and thereby releasing passion for the present moment. Here, a gem for me is "Six-Beat Bars:"

> at night I feel
> myself falling
> from a vertigo
> of being
> one step into
> the abyss and
> anxiety becomes
> my new mantle[.]

Today, the savagery of the world highlights the most important quality of life: love. Arlice W. Davenport's *Traces of the Holy* is one elaborate, bejeweled love letter to the world and all that shimmers beyond it.

—Emília Katriňáková, award-winning poet from Bratislava, Slovakia

MANDATE
In Lieu of a Preface

Stone knows the blows
of the sculptor's awl.

A shower of strokes,
and an incarnation of vision
breaks loose. Blue veins stain
the marble surface.
They flatten smoother
than curves in a human face,
squeamish in the closeness
of their love.

Art for our sake; this is
the viewer's mandate:
a future encased in white.
One smudge swallows
all shadows. Light paints an eye
for empathy on our brows,
woos the shirts off our backs,

warms our minds
to the goodness
of stone.

ALSO BY ARLICE W. DAVENPORT

Setting the Waves on Fire (Meadowlark Press, 2020)

Everlasting: Poems (Meadowlark Poetry Press, 2021)

Kind of Blue: New Poems (Meadowlark Poetry Press, 2022)

In Search of the Sublime (Meadowlark Poetry Press, 2023)

TRACES OF THE HOLY

Poems by
Arlice W. Davenport

Meadowlark Poetry Press, LLC
meadowlarkbookstore.com
P.O. Box 333, Emporia, KS 66801

Traces of the Holy
Copyright © Arlice W. Davenport, 2025

All rights reserved. This book or any portion thereof may not be reproduced or used in any manner whatsoever without the express written permission of the author, except for the use of brief quotations in a book review.

No AI Training: Use of this work to "train" generative artificial intelligence (AI) technologies is expressly prohibited. All rights to license this work for generative AI training and development of machine learning language models are reserved.

Cover Art: *Variation with Color Fields* by Norman Carr, 2020, oil on canvas, 14" x 11"
Cover Design: Norman Carr and Laura Davenport
Interior Design: Linzi Garcia, Meadowlark Press
Interior author photo taken by Laura Davenport, 2024 Local Authors Day at Wichita Public Library
Back cover author photo taken by Laura Davenport at Royal Gorge, Colorado

POETRY / American / General
POETRY / Subjects & Themes / Nature
POETRY / Subjects & Themes / Places

Library of Congress Control Number: 2025944883

ISBN: 978-1-956578-79-9

FOR LAURA, AS ALWAYS

*In love I become you, grasp the grace of your
infinity. Love goes on forever because it is never
itself. When I touch your eyes, they are mine.
When I brush your lips, they are mine, and I am you.
Together, we fall upward. We rise like fog
in the morning sun. Soon, we will be nothing
but mist. Soon, nothing but the memory of mist.
We live backward, shaped by the past's caress.
On the horizon, nothing but love becomes love.*

HYMN FOR HÖLDERLIN
By Way of an Introduction

1.
A wounded depth of sorrow
    sustains our lament.
The divine radiance is
    extinguished;
ancient gods have turned their
    backs.

All earthly abodes found
    wanting
in the dim twilight of history's
unfolding of the Logos.

And we are left hanging
in the age of the world's dark night.
Long is the turning this side of the light.

2.
The remoteness of the Holy
discloses its presence;
traces of it uttered
in the voice of faithful poets.

The calm recollection by those
who are most daring summons
the strength of surpassing,
an openness to the ineffable.

And with the inward
force of poetry,
all is preserved.

CONTENTS

TRACES OF THE HOLY: IN THE WORLD

The Clearing Where Poems Speak // 3
In Search of Lost Light // 4
Other Worlds // 6
Let Us Bring Down the House // 7
A Crooked Nail // 8
Cottonwoods // 9
The Labyrinth of Love // 10
Journey // 11
Saint Peter's, Rome // 12
Circle Back // 13
Another Breath Until I Sail // 14
Crossroads // 15
Such Stuff as Dreams Are Made On // 16
I Cast My Lot With the Infinite Sky // 17
Byodo-In Temple // 18
Awake and Listen // 19
Zion National Park // 20
A Candle for the Mortal One // 21
And Then the Rains Came // 22
New Marshes // 24
Night Vision // 26
The Unprotected Shore // 27
No Regrets // 29
The Harmony of Sky // 31
English Pastoral // 32
The Cost of Aging // 34
In the Shadows // 35
Burden of the Sun // 37

Homecoming // 38
Birthday Poem // 39
The Enigma of the Past // 40
A Taste of the Sky // 41
Contrast // 42

TRACES OF THE HOLY: WITHIN THE SELF

The Double // 45
Who Paints the Breeze // 46
Varnish // 47
This Trail Leads Nowhere // 48
A Line in the Sand // 50
Into the Mystic // 51
Moonlight // 52
Lightning // 53
Emerald Lakes // 54
Freedom to Fall // 55
The Way to the Sky // 56
When the Curtain Falls // 58
My Disappearing Path // 59
Being Human // 61
An Open Field // 62
Do Not Strive to Abide // 63
Planting // 64
Light Among the Ruins // 65
Space // 66
Lyre // 67
I Trace the Unsaid Name of Being // 68
The Rain in the Trees // 69
Answer Back // 71

Monsoon // 73
Every Color of the Desert // 75
A Poet's New Year's Eve // 76
I Swallow the Light // 77
Descartes Redux // 78
I Will Wrap Myself in Blue // 79
Quixote // 80
The Poet of Lost Causes // 81

TRACES OF THE HOLY: AT THE HEIGHTS

A Fiefdom of Words // 85
How to Write a Poem // 86
Dying for Love // 88
Because We Are Too Menny // 89
Stones // 91
Only Walking Makes the Path // 92
I Pour the Royal Wine // 94
Until Only Colors Exist // 95
Wilderness // 96
Love Never Dies // 98
A Question of Magnitude // 99
This Blue-Green Rock // 101
The Emptiness Within // 102
First Do No Harm // 104
Gravity // 105
I Am You You Are Me // 106
Life's Human Face, Human Grace // 107
Other Nutrients Nourish Me Now // 108
These Dark Shores // 109
Ascent // 110

The Book of Water // 111
Now We Rise Skyward // 112

TRACES OF THE HOLY: FOR THE DYING

I Rise to the Sky // 117
Inferno // 118
I Will Guard My Dreams // 119
We Eat; Therefore, We Are // 120
The Burden of Nothingness // 121
To Walk or Rest // 123
I Widen the Map's X // 124
Every Angel Is Terror // 125
Desert Elegy // 127
Grass Dance // 128
This Shadowland // 130
Ghosts // 131
Immortality // 132
Satisfaction // 133
A Good Soldier at His Post // 134
The Pose of the Dead // 135
Six-Beat Bars // 136
A Coat of Molten Bark // 138
And So Nature Glides By // 139
Epicurean Delights // 140
The Water Turned Hope // 141
Death Mask // 142

About the Author // 145
Acknowledgments // 146
Notes // 147

TRACES OF THE HOLY: IN THE WORLD

"The inner being of the world
often appears clouded
and hidden, and people's minds
are full of doubts . . .
but splendid nature
cheers up their days,
And doubt's dark questions
stay distant."

—Friedrich Hölderlin

The Clearing Where Poems Speak

tall grasses sting my shins
strike like broods of vipers
sinking their fangs
into the little fat left
on my brittle legs

I slice through the field
intent on the house on the horizon
it sits like a battleship of the plains
ready to scoop up UA sailors
lost in the thicket of these grasses

chlorophyll soaks into my clothes
the green smell of magic at work
beneath the beneficent sun
fire burns plants into brilliant life
if only we could live on light

how many leagues will it take
before this sea voyage ends
how many miles in tall grasses
to find the clearing where poems speak
I listen to the diction of cicadas

dusk brushes the tops of the stems
green has faded to blue to black
in the infinite reach of night
it leads me nowhere but here
where I begin and belong and bellow

In Search of Lost Light

> *Because I could not stop for Death—*
> *He kindly stopped for me—*
> *The Carriage held but just Ourselves—*
> *And Immortality.*
> —Emily Dickinson

1.
the fiddle-leaf plant stretches
to embrace my lamp light
brightness and heat stir
the plant's vital urge
to expand to move to conquer
the force of circumstance
that shackles it in soil

broad and long its leaves
shade my reading chair
they wave like fans
from antiquity languidly
pushing air into
my perspiring face
a balm of coolness

2.
I dig beside my beloved's grave
searching for her shadow
the dark yields no form no line
nothing but a black field
that absorbs my loss of vision
my quixotic quest for light

twilight spreads its maternal wings
over the woods where I wait
along the path a coach is sure to pass

its lanterns will shine in my eyes
one alert and able one dead to itself
defeated I refill the hole at her grave
lie near its edge and imbibe my dreams

Other Worlds

my verses weep to commune
with other worlds
other words of other poets
who drink blue wine
buoyant in the chalice
who pin couplets onto sestinas
stitch similes into stanzas
who climb the dark rungs of Being
as imagery morphs into metaphor
this is that / that is this

I pull on a fedora and woolen overcoat
prop my collar against the gale
when did existence turn so chilling
when will solitary lips lock in a kiss
of innocence lost / innocence regained

spirit is universal it warms us
each night in this fragile sack of skin
with it I can feel how deeply another dies
how our roots mesh like screens patched
        into broken-down doors
don't let them slam shut don't let poverty of faith
shame you / somewhere you'll find a beatitude

spirit is all we have / that and the freedom to weep
over the furthest reaches of tragedy
sprouting like blue veins atop an old man's hands
let us celebrate the freedom to cry *yes! yes!*
to inhabit other worlds
to climb the wall of meaning before
kicking away our ladder to the sun

Let Us Bring Down the House

I would count the rings but the abacus is broken
gouged-out stumps of twin sycamores litter
the yard / jagged saw-sweeps cut into the life
of urban nature / trees dressed up as trees
snow dapples the lawn with patches of gauze

I register wounds of the world / they quietly
    ooze
beneath the crust of culled woodlands /
    each arbor
hides the secret of straight and tall longevity
upper reaches of canopies brush clean
    the detritus
of dawn / she rides a white horse over
    the passes

I have pounded the paths of peace
    and harmony
until they unfurl as gouache / a touch more
water and they run like a debutante's tears
prophesy the unexpected end of happiness
tiptoe across fields of rugged shades of green

the hours of night convene to take their leave
from this tawdry makeshift stage / footlights
switch on / actors practice familiar lines / birth
life death the coming apocalypse / let us bring down
the house with its rings of solitude and joy

A Crooked Nail

I snap the plank in two.
Its ragged edge leaks
a hardened sap, inert
from eons of sleep.
I am pleased when
I touch it and nothing
sticks to my hand.

How clean nature becomes
under the weight
of a well-worn plane.
I press hard against
the knotty surface.
Leafless limbs morph
into malleable boards.

I hammer them in place, reinforce their corners,
and delight in the drip
    drip drip
of their life force. I tear my shirt on a crooked nail.
My arm stings and bleeds.
I am revived.

Cottonwoods

screen doors slam
old men slouch
in straight-back chairs
dogs circle the yard
purple-gray clouds mount
behind the chicken house
across the road
mean storms brew

I lean back against
the sharp-edged porch steps
and listen for the key
to the bewildering
morass of adult speak
welcome or not
their world shapes my own
but I understand only images

I steer clear of the shaggy ditch
full of unseen serpents
slithering through tall grass
each step a danger
beyond my reckoning
peril abounds
I seek security within
these lazy Boston Mountains

what rises above
the humid plane hides
all that brings me joy
I thirst for *entrée* to another world
far from these roots that strangle me
I am sustained by the city
near the corner of my urban lawn
cottonwoods woo me home

The Labyrinth of Love

geckos climb the wall
their tails entwined
like vines in the sun
green tendrils thick
and strong encircle
my love my wants my all

the sun paints the wall
in speckled shadows
darkness and light tie
themselves into knots
a rope tossed
to the drowning

I cannot swim but I
dog-paddle toward you
keeping my head above
water / my feet scurrying
below the surface
they touch your arm as you pass

we are born of water
and light we rise like
doves from the ashes
of our lives in them we
scribble the poetry of life
hieroglyphs for the dead

we lock hands in a warm
embrace we look each other
in the eye see ourselves
reflected back as tiny faces
geckos climb the wall wrap us
in their green labyrinth of love

Journey

When you wander between day and night and pronounce
    them "good,"
as in the eternal hour of creation, you have passed
    the threshold
of light, you have raised your voice to outdo the silence
    of the void.
Where you belong is goodness. You are free to choose only
it. Evil does not exist, nothingness is not. Stand still and
    the cosmos swirls
around you. Rise skyward and the mystic stars brand you
    with fire.

Saint Peter's, Rome

Michelangelo's *Pietà* shrinks
behind glass
Bernini's canopy shimmers
a wavy brown

the sculptors face off
like boxers in a ring
each punch plants
a terrible dent in
white marble
a squeeze of a hip here
a dip of a head there

stone can wrinkle
like time
light emanates
from wood gilded
in geometric designs

death laps across
a mother's lap
the divine turns human
in a litany of flesh

formless blocks of stone
ascend to the dome
met by a descending dove
love bounded by love

Circle Back

You exit the cave of unknowing with the bulk
    of your possessions
on your back. The weight staggers you as darkness
    drapes your body.
You sense but cannot see what threatens
    to pin you down.
You and your burden are one.

How long have you been like this? How many nights
    have you sworn to unload your things,
leaving all but your hopes behind?
This trail circles back on itself, an ouroboros
    choking on its tasteless tail.

Another Breath Until I Sail

The sleeping wind turns on its side, coughs, tousles
    my hair. I drink
its cool touch on my face. I taste the oil of olive
    groves, sun-soaked
fields. Beyond the brown hills of Priego de Córdoba,
    I project my fate.
Nothing stirs my emotions as do these dusty plains
    of Spain. I join
without joining. I bury my roots in porous soil. I find
    my home beaming
toward this outpost. Another breath until I sail
    over the arbor forever.

Crossroads

at last at this cold crossroads
I search for a faded sign
pointing to Paradise
broken it bobs in the wind
a signifier without significance

left right ahead I squirm
with uncertainty
my steps the path to the future
they leave no trace
no face to recognize as my own

I reach for the hand of my guide
but he has vanished in the woods
a shadow kingdom teeming
with dapples of light but no clear
way forward no trail home

paralyzed with uncertainty I nudge
myself onward
my gait straight as virtue
now in the midst of turmoil
I trust
the inward light of poetry
verse radiates the heat of the sun

Such Stuff as Dreams Are Made on

We are such stuff as dreams are made on;
and our little life is rounded with a sleep.
—William Shakespeare

the door to my dream swings shut
I am manacled to a tale of sorrow
nowhere to turn nowhere to fly

within my dream of a dream joy
lies hidden a god thirsting for libations
when I turn in my sleep my chalice spills

storms build above the island
the sea releases clouds like smoke
dark and threatening they rise

I wrestle the tempest to the deep
it rears up like the angel wounding Jacob
only this pain in my hip holds me down

rain ricochets off my head dousing the sky
I dig a cave for shelter but my dream demurs
its door locked I settle on prayer for the drowned

in the world *I am* escapes me only actions persist
I unlatch the door step gingerly into the fray
it grips my wrist yanks me into its fury I fall into
    rounded sleep

I Cast My Lot with the Infinite Sky

I dive into the distance of the day. It stretches beyond
    the end of the meadow, absorbed in light.
Honeysuckle perfumes my path.
Here in the Gypsum Hills, I cast my lot with
    the infinite sky.

It embraces my lonely stance. Though mute,
it speaks to me as a long-lost son. Do I recognize
its diction? Do I feel its open gift? The way caves in
on itself. I surface and breathe.

Byodo-In Temple

the gong reverberates infinity
across a neon lawn
spotted koi swarm the pond
a feeding fury

wooden chimes rattle
like bones clank melodies
in the breeze
breathe in breathe out

peace bears no color
no weight no nudging
toward the brass voice
and its endless vibrato

I wander the temple grounds
carry water on my back
move like wind gusts that ruffle
a monk's saffron robe

Awake and Listen

I dip my hand in a mountain stream
icy clear a terrible swift sword
slicing corners off tumbled stones
I gather the shavings burn them
in the quickening night

the quick and the dead loiter
in a virgin forest pull apart
pine cones sticky with sap
I gather the fragments then shape them
into a silhouette of trees

my silhouette droops with age
a fallen brow unruly hair
a nose sniffing the incense of life
I gather the resinous smell
squeezing out all perfume

her perfumed hair leads me
to the tent flashlights dancing
like marionettes on invisible strings
I drink the thinning snowmelt
anoint my head with cold

silence rules its fiefdom like an anointed
feudal lord still eager to collect taxes
from his broken hoard of serfs
I scratch a message on a piece of bark
awake and listen for the still small voice

Zion National Park

the canyon holds its breath
and I am crushed between
its walls squeezing through
the narrows / ribs bent by stone

I move only forward
carrying the weight of hope
deep within this foggy valley
steeped in the great unknown

ravens circle shallow pools of rain
fresh scars from flash floods
rapids indifferent to our humanity
swift currents deaf to our cries

red rocks rise above me
their faces creased by time
their bulk bullying mine
I would sleep under them

but my pack is pelted by rain
we drown in our desires
waiting on the western wind
wanting more than sky can hold

no turning back now only one way forward
I traipse the anxious pilgrim's trail
scaling summits with no descent
each foothold a step into eternity

every taste of victory turns cold
how I hunger for the sun
and its life-changing rays how I murmur
as I count my days / each breath a vise of pain

A Candle for the Mortal One

Nevermore will I pin Poe's longings on the Raven. Dressed in sleek, shiny ebony, it sits erect on a branch staring into nothing. Thus quoth the Raven, "Nevermore." Yet the bird is drenched in immortality; it now transcends the work of Poe and his addicted admirers. The Raven returns, and the one who has tasted death lights a candle.

And Then the Rains Came

1.
She stands transfixed
before tall corn shocks.
Giant green crowns
rustle in the breeze.
Fat, yellow kernels
glisten with flavors.
The good earth ushers
in new life to nourish
the old. I take steps
toward my ghostly
grandmother, watch
her cotton-print dress
drape my view. I await
nature's success
in the sun. I strip cobs
of excess tassels.
The fragrance
of renewal overwhelms.

2.
Before now, I would hide
among the stalks,
stacking them
into impenetrable
fortresses, my mouth
watering like
an afternoon
shower ready
to burst into
the night's monsoon.

3.
I knew nothing then
about the seasons, sowing

and reaping, the register
of hunger filling
my empty head
with rows of pain.
I imagined invaders,
crashing through
the green, triggering
my adrenaline. *O when
will we dine al fresco
on these yellow cobs?*

4.
Let us drown our
impatience in the rain-
soaked tides. Let us
paint our faces like
lighthouses of spirit.
Their gleams break
into blossoms,
into colors so rich
the soil turns
green with envy.

5.
Pat down the kernels,
add seasoning, butter,
and the shadow
of Earth. Let all
who crave
the sweet sensation
bow their heads to
the sun. It burns only
for a moment, then
fires salvos of flavor,
ghosts of smoke rising
to verdant fields above.

New Marshes

I cannot raise this burden
off your back. My arms
no longer lift;
my spine shoots bullets of pain.
Like Judas and his soiled silver,
my body betrays me
with a kiss.

Eons from now, I will not
remember this moment.
Its watershed losses will
drown in details from a new yesterday.
Nothing lasts,
least of all significance.
I project myself
into the future, live it out
only as the present.
Pure consciousness nihilates
realms of Being.

They slosh against my legs
as I slog my way
through sticky marshes.
Each step suctions up
sections of quicksand.
I rise only to sink back
in the viscous mess
of nature's corpuscles and veins.

No place transforms wishes
into shining deeds.
I pause to eat and sleep,
tracing signatures

in the sky, cirrus circles
float aimlessly.

Soon I see a way forward,
leading to history's courtroom.
I will be judged insufficient,
then stab my thigh
for life-giving blood.

Night Vision

With eyes as large as frying pans,
two great horned owl toddlers
watch me stumble into the dark canyon.
Abandoned at dusk, I sense their stares
piercing my back. I suck in my breath,
squeeze through the strait gate
of pale, smooth stone.

The owls ponder my strangeness.
Seeing no trace of food, they roost.
They are whole beyond measure,
awaiting their mother with the night's kill.
I touch the air she cleaves. It tells me
I am exiled from my perch, forever fixed
in the all-consuming dark.

The Unprotected Shore

Heavy with drowning dreams,
the sea ravages the shore:
a battery of breaking waves.
Crabs scurry above the tide,
skimming sideways to shelter.
A rider and horse in fleet
pursuit. Irresistible wind,
sand gorging the twilight,
each flick of the mane
a metronome of joy.

I follow at my
steady pace, one leg
longer than the other,
one way only to advance.
No rearview mirror
of regret. No taste
of immortality. Is this
freedom, peace, the pinnacle
of discovery? Do I sail
into the age of adventure?

Thrown one time too many,
I no longer ride. I glide
through the clouds
like a spring shower.
All creation doused
in warm water.
I stop above a dead
starfish, pink flesh
as alluring as
berries and cream.

A gull will delight
in it, then bully others.
No footprints behind me.
I keep walking, ever hopeful,
into the wind.

No Regrets

1.
I rise early, escape the house.
The air is cool, clear, untouched.
Warmth stirs, rises, and retreats.
It will arrive, full force, midafternoon.

In the distance, a blue mirage of mountains
wraps around my grandparents' farm.
Cornfields tower over me, cover
my path eastward. Another step,

and I will reach the clearing. No one
else stirs until birds whistle and cry.
And so the day begins, without
pretense, promise, or play.

2.
I am aimless, restive, stuck
between strands of barbed wire.
One wrong move, and I risk
shredding my back, my mind.

I carry little with me. I latch
onto dreams, still amorphous,
still tricking my eyes into seeing
what once was, but now has died.

Before my brother passed, he asked me
to spread his ashes on the mountainsides.
I objected to his cremation, but he insisted
his sick body was not worth preserving.

3.
The sun at last crests the peaks. I spy
formations on the summit: hikers turning
witlessly. If only they knew whose bodies
they trampled. If only ashes could scream.

When shadows fall, my vision narrows to a thin,
black line. *Before* and *after* blur into an inchoate
now. I dwell in it as if on my final journey.
The way, fraught with peril, remains unknown.

At nightfall, I will rouse from my bed and scour
the countryside for signs of revelation, direction,
the intimate whisper to turn 'round and repent.
No regrets, I told my brother. He nodded, grinned,
    then violently coughed.

The Harmony of Sky

You could write a poem about
the force of failure, how it blows
down the hut you huddled in,
how the mud walls you smoothed
crumble in the wind. But the pink
dawn hails your choice to walk free,
to soak up the peace of forests,
the harmony of sky, the color
of the Earth's new turning. Transform
your pen into a brush. Paint the face
you deserve. Don't forget the wrinkles
and spots. Claim the beauty
that is yours: Recovery swims
in the darkest well. Let it splash you
with hope. Let it cradle you in love.

English Pastoral

the iron gate shrieks open
like a mouse in a sticky trap
I rewrite the end of my journey
passing over a rickety stile
planted halfway downfield
sheep meander heads low
cattle cast silhouettes
against a mottled sky

there is no retracing
my steps here
I shake off
the lassitude of the day
stride through
the fence's opening
drop my hat on a patch
of dry ground then rest
amid green pastures
silent but teeming
with uncut jewels

this way ends where
it begins *en medias res*
thrown into the world
we skate past the pitfalls
of vanity insecurity
the seven deadly sins
we plot a rendezvous
deep on the other side
I record the minutes
of our last meeting
divide them by quiet
conversations
who says much
says nothing at all

an ancient road sign
brays *Lower Slaughter
2.5 miles ahead*
lazing but planted firmly
by the river and into

the elephant-skin bark
of an ancient oak
unimpeded on its way
to the sheltering sky

The Cost of Aging

I bounce into a silver-globe whirlpool
spinning on the Colorado River.
Moss stains the water. Green sprints
up steps to the sun: heat, light,
iridescence. I cannot grasp what defies
nature. Only the organic roots of flora
nestle in my grip. I would weave a headdress
of earth tones, wear it on high days of sacrifice.
Soil stains the horizon, free of colors, free of limits.
To be born is but our first move, caught in the devil's
    bargain.

In the Shadows

1.
Born in shadow, the boy I was
spies the sunny, just-mown lawn
through the living room window.

He is reading, as usual, trying
to sustain the high of literature's
thrilling mountain summits.

From Hemingway to Cummings,
he learns how to invoke the word
that swallows all words but his own.

Imitation is not the highest flattery.
It is a rite of humility, hoping to be
what the author has become: ideal.

Existence makes no distinction
among its modes: in a flowery page
of James or the Utes' red rock lands.

2.
The boy scuffs his boots on the trail
that slinks away from the silent corral.
Ahead, a shadowy butte beckons.

An aura of power electrifies
the desert floor. The Earth shakes
its head at the naivete of humans.

They risk being lost in a realm
not their own to discover a mystical
link to poets from other worlds.

The boy's poems circle himself. *I want, I want, I want* all that he does not have. I retreat to the shadows. Will I find him there?

Burden of the Sun

The hills sweat a rust-colored blood
    as the patriarchal sun
bears down on them. I seep through shadows,
    my pack taut
with poems. Somewhere, I will gather holy rocks
    to ventilate
my dreams at dusk. Soon, they will deliver me
    to the life I am
fated for. It haunts me like a breath of frigid air
    from the stars.
My only defense: to bury myself in rays
    of rust-colored light.

Homecoming

The moon spills its luminous jewels along the side
of the road. Light dapples the rocks that splay across
grassy knolls. I am walking toward home, ever
receding, ever near, mirage of the night, black hole
of hopes and dreams. I touch the light behind its closed
doors, taste citrus in the wind. My mouth
waters at the thought. Why have I left? What awaits
beyond the crest of the hills? I stumble on a stone.
My eyes water at the pain.

Birthday Poem

stuck in the final stage of my seventieth year
I use the words of my birth to stir
my lust for living
the phrases still sound fresh
the notes of my symphony ring clear
an abiding love absorbs all dissonance

light filters through the shades of my room
ray after ray shimmers in the window pane
they land on faces of a family portrait
they carom off walls and cling to corners
their sharp angles press into my flesh
pain seeps like sap from a winter birch

what comes in the night
cautiously comes but once
I sense it behind me panting
I send it packing into indigo spheres
so many are missing from this comedy of errors
they exit the stage like sheep in a fog

dark forces advance down the hallway
they enliven the sun slip past the moon
angels wield flaming swords
unlike them I exist nowhere but here
east of Eden's exile suits me fine
I have learned my lines for its final act

The Enigma of the Past

1.
Stubborn as a mule, the past
demands keepsakes
from my memory, tiny jewels

encrusted on velvet pillows,
too precious to be worn,
too bright to be seen.

I wear only one ring: gold, scarred
by duels at twenty paces. Behold:
the resurrected poet.

2.
I have jettisoned my past as flotsam,
but it returns, an insidious intruder,
like the hidden moon pushing high tide.

I have sailed after Neptune,
his trident flashing, his mane flowing,
steeled to fight his foes under waves.

Seawater leaves a sticky brine.
Bathe in it and you are never clean.
Your faults will glisten like gold.

3.
Or so I remember . . . The past keeps
insisting. It wrangles my mind, forcing
me to flee this search for lost time.

A Taste of the Sky

And so I became a tree,
subterranean roots snaking
through the dark toward a living
patch of rain. How I plunged
my body into it, wrapping
cells in sandy soil.
I dreamt of one thing only:
the taste of the sky, its azure
mantle tempting me to soar
above a pack of saplings
who ridicule my Old World
ways. But old is new, new
is old. Buds burst into view
along the breadth of my branches.
I will break into blossom,
I said, taking the poet's dictum
to embrace the sun, marry the moon,
make my homestead among
the birds, whose songs wake
the dawn in blessed
cacophony. Like them, I am
an expressionist, emotions
dry in my bark, scars
crown my brown-green
color fields. Nothing grows
but love for what is.
I laugh and taste the sky.
It is salty and warm,
just as my father promised.

Contrast

Fingers of dawn claw through blackened veils
    of night.
Light emerges from the Herculean weight of the sun.
It sags with the heaviness of Heaven.
All that rises rebukes gravity, takes its cues
from the shrill cry of gulls,
whose gold-doubloon eyes refract
the thickness of things.

I take refuge in caves on the storm-beaten beach.
I must hide in shadow, free from the threat of fire.
Released, I scale the ladder of vapors that leads
    to my perch among the stars.
Do I belong where I land? Do I strain to hurl
Sisyphus' stone into these celestial spheres?

I fashion a handful of sand into an effigy of Neptune.
He rides the waves like an expert horseman.
One tug of the reins and night reasserts its will.
The sky is a black hole swallowing all that shifts
    its shape toward day.
I have forsaken color in my gray-fog vision.
I see only contrast; it drives me on.

TRACES OF THE HOLY: WITHIN THE SELF

"All the fruit is ripe,
plunged in fire, cooked,
And they have passed
their test on Earth,
and one law is this:
That everything curls inward . . .
dreaming on the hills of heaven."

—Friedrich Hölderlin

The Double

my doppelgänger digs his grave
I stalk him as each shovelful
slingshots back to Earth
in the beginning is our end
in our end the beginning

how close to the tree we fall
clinging to our high-altitude origins
we fly before we grow
we peel away layers
of the sky its azure dome riddled
with pinpoints of light

I dance on the coffin's lid
pressing each nail into place
sealed against the anarchy of life
my double's roadblocks turn to rocky detours
I skin my knee against stone
my blood flows as his blood
spilling into an anemic pool

he rustles the canopy of leaves
whimpering like an adolescent coyote
in search of prey / he doubles all my debts
but never pays / he courts romantic love
only to shrink from the lover's touch
why must I see through his eyes

I shall dream this night away / the breath of time
stirs the embers of my fire as he warms
his bones beside me I find only darkness
in his face / he will soon steal my clothes
ruin my voice and pray for another soul
to emerge from Dante's ninth circle of Hell

Who Paints the Breeze

a stand of oaks sambas
in the breeze / they whisper
the important thing is *to move*
we hurl ourselves up the hillside
scattering clods and stones
beneath a translucent sky

who saw our struggles then
who wrote the poem about young love
and its endless stages of belief
I say the *coup de grâce* is *to be*
to sink satisfied and safe
into the soil to smear mud on our faces
to not wash until the fledgling wrinkles crack
into a fractured spider's web

when we lassoed the trees pulling them tight
the evening limned us as lost children of light
now I see dimly only what's set before me
my *joie de vivre* lies buried beneath a mound
    of quilts
I grasp what shimmers in the dark and by its glow
bow to the one who paints the breeze

Varnish

I strip varnish from the dark-wood paneling
shellac peels away to reveal planks of knotty pine
with sticky hands I contemplate the new order

in a corner stands an upright piano plastered
with sheet music the paper has faded yellow
shaped notes spell out a Chopin nocturne

the Polish maestro mesmerizes with his playing
such passion elevates my mood beyond itself
a captive of the outermost reaches of Paradise

paroxysms of power and joy ripple through the air
I am exhilarated to carry on along this pilgrim path
existential illumination rises from unvarnished keys

This Trail Leads Nowhere

a mirage of mercy shimmers
above the two-lane highway
asphalt heatwaves rise
on a blistering summer day
I reach to touch their fiery edges
to feel the warmth of a life
disappearing beyond
the brass horizon

I am that life slipping through
my fingers like sand in the desert
tiny lizards flit past my tent
they taunt me with their freedom
I wear the shackles of choice
which weigh down my wanderings
rain is my only manna forty days without
forty nights within still no moisture

to slake my thirst I hunt the dew
collect its transparent droplets
pour them into my cup like
agèd wine how sweet the taste
of earth how it lingers
on the palate the ever-present
coating of soil a finish of blood
dust to dust ashes to ashes

I must go on I can't go on I will go on
this trail leads nowhere a labyrinth
within a labyrinth / settle on the center
and you must start again stepping off
into infinity reaching for the summit
of some stumpy mountain

peak experiences spontaneously
combust then implode under water

tonight my mind is hollow I dream
of explosions of color a touch of red
in this lifeless terrain / let it burn

A Line in the Sand

I draw a line in the sand
that the tide cannot cross
ahead breakers crash
against a deadly harbor
of basalt pyramids
behind starfish struggle
to breathe as their pink flesh burns

my footprints leave no trace
gulls pick at larger pebbles
kick away the detritus of the sea
the purple-pink horizon
spreads its arms to embrace
every possibility of flight
I pull my albatross closer

poetry cannot be heard
in the roar of the waves
they rise up like cobras
dancing to the moon's
magic flute they flare
their gills before they strike
only one more bite and I will be
immune to their poison

I will rest as the stars climb
the rungs of the dark
my line in the sand now invisible
the need to possess the distance
but a folly of the dispossessed
belonging is like the art of losing
you realize what you had was not your own
but it is too late to give it back

Into the Mystic

this paradise is not perfection
tear up your poem scatter its petals
on the brook that flows
    past suffering into fire and life

the self is numinous it reshapes
    the *élan vital*
it contemplates death in the restless night
it shoulders dread like a one-armed pack
it stuffs its bag full of time space and flesh
it fights mortality like an agonist of spirit

the way forward points downward forever
    falling
immersed in dark waters drawing sustenance
from dark roots buried in the earth
charge them as luminous let us learn to live on light

the living flame of love burns away
all dross of resentment you must find
the transcendent in the immanent
you must float the currents of ripeness
    until they decay

the dying are born into light
they touch the fringe of the other world
in light they carve their totemic vision
of the ordinary with sharp white stones

they know Orphic moments
they know the *via negativa* they achieve
mystical union they burn like wildfires
they produce no ash

Moonlight

fronting Adriatic swells
ruins of a medieval castle
tower behind me
a cyclops of stone

with my one good eye
I watch the future unfurl
like a tidal wave
crashing the shore

I can no longer swim
the oceanic sky
a blue as deep as
my heaving breath

history numbers each
building block of time
I search for my birth year
but find only hieroglyphs

within my reach
gems of the past
glisten like morning dew
I hammer them into dust

balancing on the sea floor
I dance like Dionysus
into the frenzied night
moonlight guides my way

Lightning

a jay bounces in his bath
batters tepid waters
washes feathers clean

around him sycamores die
mute victims of lightning
shedding burned-out bark

I imagine creosote and freight cars
crossing an empty junction
tired markers clatter and flame

nature defies time births offspring
in the spring then turns bloody tyrant
    and murders its own

the trees will come down
a naked backdrop for the jay
I cleanse my sadness in tepid waters

Emerald Lakes

Pansies beam beside pale, wide stones.
Emotion is born of longing.
How I yearn for the colors of youth,
the gold of fertile wheat fields,
the green of ancient trees in spring.

Sadness falls across my path,
its shadow sprawls behind me.
If I stop to look, I will return to the earth,
devour grubs, flap my arms,
crash into a tangle of bracken.

Walking turns my steps into silent markers.
They plot the way to emerald lakes,
a verdant sanctuary for tired geese,
who beat their wings against the sky,
and laugh at humans passing by.

Freedom to Fall

cobblestones glisten in the mist
I slip and slide across
    their slick surfaces
only the incline frightens me
to fall as I climb would cue
    a chorus of ridicule

I try walking backward
but my heels are caught
    in creases of stone
I pitch forward into packs
of pilgrims ascending
to the sacred throne

the cathedral exhales incense
otherworldly aromas pool
    in the crest of the dome
I catch my breath disoriented
    from the climb unable to feel
    the fire of the divine

Spain licks its wounds of fascism
    and inquisitions / its hold over me
    an incorrigible love of the divine
in the mundane machinations
    of the Mass I eat and drink
    my freedom to forever fall

The Way to the Sky

1.
white desiccated gnarled by death
another hollow branch of the sycamore
cracks its way to earth
pops and scatters
brittle leaves turn prematurely yellow
line their sapless resting place

lightning strikes twice
twin trees burned side by side
still standing
still hardening their core
against molting bark
they are motionless prey
simmering in the acrid smell of decay

2.
my hand rests on the desk
gnarled and sore its bones
harden into stone
its joints ache with fire
the desolation of aging

still I type the words of art
the dictates of poetry
direct my movements stir my mind
to touch the other world of symbols
signs and sighs of desperation

I write but The Word is not made flesh
its sign points everywhere and nowhere
the path is made by walking
walking is made by the path

each step rebounds in its shadow
substance thins to an existential gruel
we sip from an open manger

3.
I climb the broken limbs
reach high toward the sky
lasso the clouds
lacerate my dreams
stitch the pieces into tapestries
of yearning and delight

I hover in midair
between Heaven and Earth
each ascension recoils
caught by gravity
coerced by the facile laws
of physics

soon the trees will be toppled
their stumps ground into dust
the dust scattered on the lawn
the lawn bursting to new life

tall shafts of grass will rise in protest
of the presumptions of death
its appetite to destroy
all that laughs in its face
with the fire of life

let us burn these dead branches
until they light the way to the sky

When the Curtain Falls

streets simmer soaked in sweat
summer tightens its grip as leaves turn
into sprays of opulent colors / a hue
for every mood / they cut like a knife

blood on the tracks / locomotives barrel past
the fringe of the city / they spark short-lived fires
that smolder under the weight of heat's retreat
I turn up my collar memorizing my lines
    for autumn

an actor on the stage of Ibsen's *Ghosts*
I stride back and forth on the dusty boards
the soles of my feet flap an ugly gray
they slap me with recalcitrant force

when the curtain falls my mood will shed its sweat
winter's early breezes will freeze my neck
I search for my coat dark in a closet
how can misery reign amid such beauty
I pluck a leaf pin it to my chest

My Disappearing Path

> *Travelers, there is no path.*
> *Paths are made by walking.*
> —Antonio Machado

coffee cup on the table
stares back at me
I am a marvel a creature
who moves and thinks
and speaks in a foreign tongue
if only I could bridge the gap
between this forlorn object
and my formless freedom

I cannot choose not to choose
I pick up the cup drain its contents
lukewarm and bitter
a one-way connection
like words on a page
white fibers cannot contain
the shifting shape of dreams
I hear Machado laughing behind me

nothing matters but beauty
I breathe it in exhale a moan
then bury my desires in the mindless muck
    of a world turned rogue
to say that I am solitary and inward
is but an existentialist cliché
who isn't in the wee wee hours
who doesn't turn and turn in a faceless crowd

poetry yearns to become an *objet d'art*
forever fixed in the stratosphere
flickering like a newborn star

we die charting the sky and its infinite jest
metaphor makes a sorry dwelling place
room only for two well-worn bags
I carry mine upon my back
Machado cackles at my disappearing path

Being Human

1.
Bernini's sculptures strain
behind marble masks
fountains batter our senses
cast their arms around us
squeezing harder
ever jealous of our love

never has Piazza Navona
    been so empty
never have the statues' backs
    burned green with envy
never have we ogled their forms
    for a trace of being human

2.
to live as stone stifles all yearning
better to drown with a slim volume
of *Pisan Cantos* in our pocket
flutes of champagne in hand
and so we read and toast read and toast
bestowing honor on Roman ghosts

I see nothing but your alabaster face
    beaming like a newborn moon
your searching eyes bore through me
    like drills through a mountainside
rubble rises and reassembles
    in a haven of living hope

3.
I take your hand heavy with jewels
mount the ring on your finger
the piazza beams an otherworldly light
it shadows our love for the expatriate life
we are one caught in this instance of time
as it disappears into Cupid's night

An Open Field

bramble chokes my ankles
boots powerless to clear the view
I am stuck like a child entangled
in nature's grasp
fighting for entrance
to an open field
a bobcat prowls the premises
so relaxed he cannot
track his next meal
I watch him weave
past aging fence posts
sniff the honeysuckle
that masks the void
I want to walk with him
loosen my boots
but memories
of a young boy's *then*
still suffocate my *now*

Do Not Strive to Abide

I write poems as hard as bone
windswept lyrics water them
from the sea's dark floor
then drown our trek to Carmel
I circled its tower of stone
storms roiled my mind
buried my errant pride

beauty burns
like nature's fiery force
my hands are singed
my defenses flame
under a cobalt sky
I feed them into
this elemental strife
I wrangle roan stallions
that I will never ride

swift-winged hawks
swoop above the waves
grace and beauty bind
their wildness to the winnowing sky
Jeffers' poems stir me to build
a coastal home
no human hands
can hold back the tide

beauty's poetics read
etch your heart
do not strive to abide
this is the Zen you'll practice
till the day you die

Planting

I bury a cache of darkened seeds
in a corner of the greening lawn.
They vanish in tunnels of loam, keen
to feed on the sun's seeping warmth.

My brother digs for shoots, collects
swaddling clothes of rain.
A squirrel trails him, divots of dirt
in their wake. United in want, they sigh.

He is dead now, stuck in a thicket of mortality,
mud lining his boyish face. His headstone
is cracked. Jonquils push to the sky.
My poems taste of life.

Light Among the Ruins

No one has lived here long.
The stone walls crumble.
Rubble blankets the floor.
Windows open onto woods.
I touch the missing sill of the sun
and imagine where I belong.

From the beginning, you are here.
I would scrape our initials on the wall,
but the surface cuts my hand.
How I wish the ancestors spoke
in clear, prophetic voices.
How I long for the comfort of home.

This life doubles another.
I grasp the papers on the bench.
Your handwriting spills past the edges.
I read a message from before we were.
Love infiltrates all emotion and thought.
The light of my poems lengthens near dusk.

Space

I hug the edge of the trail. Spray-painted sheep dine
    on spotted pastures.
Heads down, they hum as they rummage for moist
    morsels of green.
So many colors reduced to two. White on dirty white.
I would paint this scene if I could paint. I would
    draw these shapes on cavern walls
in ocher and black. I would occupy space
    like time, linked
to its intimate rhythms, moving with it as I breathe:
    unconscious of the sheep or trail.

Lyre

I am distant and wan, pinned down
in liminal lands of Homer and Dante.
They chanted to Apollo and Beatrice,
raised the consciousness of every living muse.
They struck a chord on the lyre,
plucked melodies
from its high-strung strings.
Blood and stardust.
How the elements infuse us.
How they tempt us with everlasting Being.
This time, I will write something worthy,
no longer a poet in name only.

I Trace the Unsaid Name of Being

I turn on the lamp as
rain rattles the rafters
this silver assault
from blackened skies

I close the book stretch
to straighten the shade
as I open the window
a warm mist bathes my wrist

I trace the unsaid name
of Being I hear the voices
drone but listening is not doing
nor empty full in my notebooks

years trickle across my path
through the garden rows
I shut the ever-banging gate
sunflowers tower over me

mud trails me to my desk
no step free of stain
I could mark my way home
but water washes us clean

tonight with no thought
of my own I sketch
an image on a page
it carries all my hopes

but only if I heed the ghost
who directs my pen
and erases my steps
into the everlasting dark

The Rain in the Trees

I find myself in the city library.
I wander the stacks
in search of nothing
but poetry. I am guided
to W. S. Merwin, a poet
unknown to me. I finger
the spine of *The Rain
in the Trees*, open
the book at random.

I devour the poem
on an odd-numbered page.
It is sublime, weep-inducing.
I think *This is how I must
write. These are my poems
in waiting*. I live with the book
for weeks. My constant companion,
it annihilates my oeuvre, picking apart
each poem like pieces of lint.

Soon, the rain falls on me,
washing away the grit
of my existential grind.
What I wish to say in my poetry
remains unknown. The rain
in the trees washes clean
my self-indulgence, rinses
away the dirt of ambition.
Am I a poet? Who decides?

Years later, I interview
Merwin by phone. He is
charming, lively, as warm

as an old friend, as full
of anecdotes about Pound
and Lowell as an ancient mariner.
Privileged, he learned from the best,
he rose on their wings,
watched their feathers fall.

I have not seen him,
but I have loved him.
His death was like a frigid
shock. Unexpected but
as natural as the rain
in the trees. I climb the maple
in my yard. Its thick limbs
support my weight. I carry
The Rain in the Trees
with me. It still breaks my fall.

Answer Back

we wake to a world
beyond all reckoning
we touch the fire
strip the birch
war strews
its bloody bundles
across the porous soil
failed crops
faded braids of glory

our love looms
like a fortress
stuffed with endless
goods ammunition
gunpowder flint
I aim the rifle
cock the hammer
squeeze the trigger
a loud click
and nothing happens
nothing ever happens
except this planet turns
and we bow down to its delicate
balances its battlements
as thick as an elephant's side

I once had time
to count the victories
notched in stone
now numbness wraps
its fingers around
my neck now I feel only
a jagged pulse

the beat of a distant drum
a song of love
that encases
my heart with fat
from an iron skillet
bang it against the birches
soon tall spirits
will answer back

Monsoon

monsoon wraps around me
like a porous cloak
I soak in its warm bath of jewels
I clutch my chest and shout for joy
water is life is cleansing
is the source of all Being
save for my mind
and inscrutable self

on the tea-blooming hills
of Darjeeling I see my father
tramping upward toward a grueling
Sunday dinner with a local family
he is a young serviceman stationed
in Calcutta where he tightens
cargo cords cuts Gordian knots
for those still captured in his caste
it is the 1940s and no one is created equal

I am repulsed by war
though it shows us the world
here no one brews such
puissant tea no one douses
the table with curry
no one offers precious meat
to such an august guest

like his hosts my father exults in the new
until everyone carries home the walls
    of silence within them
until everyone washes down their meal
    with pungent tea
    and the promise that we can stop

      the flood of death
      before it comes
I look away wipe my eyes and saunter on
all hope dies in the mothering rain
I reach for my father and he is gone

Every Color of the Desert

The painted pony shuffles out of the barn's back door
and waits for me to open the gate that leads to her
favorite pasture. She nudges the green edges,
chomps heads off the Kentucky Bluegrass
I rolled in as a child.

The pony approaches, a scout, eyeing the intruder
with an apple in his hand. When I rode a different
black-and-white at six, my knuckles turned pale
from clawing the saddle's horn, my face
screwed up in terror at the height of the pony's back.

One rough bounce,
and I would be earthbound and bruised, unfit
    to ride. But my grandfather held the reins.
He led us at a sleepwalking gait around
    the corral until my fear subsided.

Now I offer my apple, pat the paint's long nose,
ruffle her mane, rub her ears, and marvel
at the gentle strength of this beautiful, strange
creature, her coat like an abstract canvas, eyes
alive with light, staring into mine, searching for hints
    I can be trusted.

In Grandfather's gloved hands, we become one.
I wade through memory upon memory. I touch
    the hem of blanched clouds.
Beneath the tree-lined butte, I find every color
of Utah's desert in the black-and-white face

that nuzzles my hand, grants my trust,
and rolls in the hay to live again.

A Poet's New Year's Eve

I rest in the ruts of a dirt road
painting calligraphic figures
around cairns made of bones
on the hill a face ignites the moon

I count the random feathers
fallen from red hawks' tails
sky guides them upward
till currents shift in the wind

my path is lined with pages
of poems left breathing long after
critic wars and cruel fads closed
the future of free verse

when I read Cummings as a boy
I gathered enchantment like firewood
now I ask poetry to build barriers
between readers and the world

if I could sketch the light within
that settles in the crowns of trees
I would drown my homestead
in it and bury all my books

now alliteration and harmony waft
through the treetops no note unheard
slow music of the spheres
to scale the mountains of Purgatory

no sin goes unpunished even
if our hands are clean one slip
of the brush and black binds Earth
and sky / we scour our skin till it bleeds

I Swallow the Light

The Earth swells, pregnant, fecund, stretching
> beyond itself toward birth.

Only one type of human emerges: deep, obtuse,
> clairvoyant, blind.

I see beyond my own story. I grasp the rod, fling
> the hook, reel in

a stage prop for my next act. *Exit stage right.*
My wading boots drag me down. I shuffle
> to the shore. Everything reminds me of this
> struggle to exist: whole but incomplete,

lucid but inebriated. Another cast, and I
> swallow the light.

Descartes Redux

As we push and pull against each other, we cannot see how close
we've become. Sealed with a breath of the infinite, our touches shiver in the wind.
You are my right brain and my left. I am but a wisp of consciousness
wandering the cosmos. I intend the stars, *and they are there.*
I unleash the hounds, and they bay at their prey, as the sun scalds
the moon. Because we *are,* I no longer need to think at all.

I Will Wrap Myself in Blue

a windmill's silhouette quivers
in the evening breeze
azure seeps across the pond
fish stir in search of sleep

all is empty / barren branches
brush the sky / death lurks
in shadows from the east
a sigh fades on the wind

when we last pushed through
this night past sand and sedges
I took your hand steadied myself
then sprang into the sterile sky

a new Eden awaits I told myself
you blessed my dreamy moves
stole a strand of neurons pressed
them against my rope-burned neck

your hand has vanished with the leaves
its grip now slack its warmth like river rock
I would carve every inch of you in stone
memorize your body / wrap myself in blue

Quixote

driven by dissatisfaction
I dream I storm the ramparts
of *La Mancha* to capture
echoes of the ineffable

what cannot be said can be felt
the senses trade masks
at a country ball hide behind
veils of velvet and gold

no one is who they think they are
no one stands a chance
of discovery or revelation
there is no way left to be oneself

I don the helmet of Quixote
mount my nag wield my sword
the lonely plains hold no treasure
foes loom but can never be named

The Poet of Lost Causes

I peel back a corner of the sky
galaxies dance or sit out the waltz
every new day glides
into the next sparks spawn novas

when I composed my first poem
I was subject object creator
only the self mattered caught
in an orbit of ambition and dread

I have advanced to the halls
of Being both here and beyond
ever-present and vanishing into
vacant pages of unborn poems

now I spill gallons of words and signs
the burgeoning poet of lost causes
of growth and depth and decay
stealing stars along the way of the dead

TRACES OF THE HOLY: AT THE HEIGHTS

"What is all that men have done
and thought over thousands of years,
compared with one moment of love?
There all stairs lead
from the threshold of life.
From there we come, to there we go."

—Friedrich Hölderlin

A Fiefdom of Words

wrapped in scarlet the answer
arrives at my doorstep
feverishly knocking
giant pin oaks shade
the wraparound porch

lost in "The Second Coming"
I imagine Yeats conducting
an enormous search for Celtic spirits
like faeries they dance ovals on the lawn

Poetry makes nothing happen
so Auden lamented amid the mess
    on his studio floor
order is a parasite
that sucks the blood of chaos
swirling in our heads

still I write and write
and read masters of verse
their legacy mutates on the wind
caught in a dynamic red flow
from an unused altar

knocking persists annoys my muse
I ask only for the perfect metaphor
for the insight wrapped in imagery
poetry is not wisdom but twirls
a fiefdom of words into the scarlet light

How to Write a Poem

first build a fire
be renewed by its warmth
watch the smoke rise
a deep gray calligraphy
the wind scoots letters
into the shape
of your name

find a piece of charcoal
fill in the blank spaces
of smoldering earth
draw an image
add color and dimension
outline it in ashes
scatter them once
you are sure
you will not forget
their new shape

think of Ahab and the whale
the white sheet of paper in your mind
has done more than amputate your leg
it taunts you to make
something out of nothing
to alchemize your image into words
that will sink into the viscera
of your being
taking on form like a fledgling
falling to earth
from a nest
high above

soon the words will flow
like currents of air
they will float on the unseen
stir the depths
of your imagination
spur you to risk your reputation
for *le mot juste*
for the perfect phrase
that resonates
with the fire of the sun

blow the smoke into the form
of another great white whale
take aim at its broad back
tattooed with stanzas
read the first lines
then fling your harpoon
into the dark

Dying for Love

Madame Bovary drinks in romance from
    a stack of French novels
teetering on the table. Adventure, danger,
    and a life rife with promise
flood her overheated brain, flush out
    her emotions, shock her alive
to all corners of the cosmos, all sources
    of escape from the reign
of the common. She will wager everything
    to taste but a sliver of what
fiction offers. "*Le monde, c'est moi,*" she sighs,
    then takes her poison.

Because We Are Too Menny

silent on the Thomas Hardy trail
scuffing my shoes against
subterranean stones
hardship not tragedy
attends my way

his boyhood cottage
humble well-lighted
by the noonday sun
hidden beneath a frilly
bedspread the seeds
of genius germinate

Jude the Obscure
looms in the corner
patron saint of all
our progeny who hang
from a rope / their bodies
cold stiff bearing the sign
Done because
we are too menny

The Native returns across
the vacant heath
vast and threatening
because we are too menny
bracken browns
green valleys burn

I read Hardy's elegies
to his misbegotten wife
how she suffered in her attic
apart from him

how she conquered
his resistance to her death

he poured out his regrets
in poem after poem but failed
to recapture the force of their love
because his faults of a lifetime
were too menny

Stones

My father's legacy dies within me.
I carry his book of rules like a coffin with no lid.
A long, gray, wooden rectangle
full of admonition and praise,
phrases spilling out like stones
splashed with symbols and ciphers.

Stones stacked to heights below my grasp,
staging the play of ancient axioms:
Do, don't, resist.
Ahead, the future, rife with signs:
Go, stop, resist.
Resist the emptiness of death,
the ephemera of memory.

Carry stones like sins.
Pray for mercy, forgiveness.
Carry his legacy like iron
in the soul.

Weight of sorrow and disbelief.
Weight of anguish and grief.
Nothing good dies within me.

Only Walking Makes the Path

1.
There is no path.
Only walking makes the path.
One foot in front of the other.
One way forward.
Walk it like a gangplank.
You no longer swim,
your destination unknown.

There is no path. Wherever you traipse
you are there and nowhere else. You
move without moving, you consult a map
drawn in invisible ink. One more foot in front,
and you abandon the quest. Turn back
to the beginning. Like a rusted
road sign, it is battered, riddled
with bullet holes. Its post
has been swept away, crippled
by potholes in the sand.

There is no path. Nowhere to go.
You peer past the horizon for some
sign of life, some color of dusk
that brightens your spirit. You
cannot name it, but you bask
in its beams. It is the color of
belonging, clinging to the rim
of an orange-stained canyon.
Pulling yourself up to begin
again. You make the path,
then forget it.

2.
I would walk with you, sharing
the burden of the pathfinder,
the pathmaker. But you walk
alone, alienated from the world
that hems you in, that squeezes
the breath out of your aching
lungs. Another gasp and you
flop like a fish on land.
Here is your element: nothing
fixed, nothing set, nothing
moving like nothing before.

Do you show me the way?
Does your path entice,
inspire a journey through
the stars? Pinpricks of white,
they cast down codes
of home, deciphered as
an endless odyssey. The path
is but a setting on the helm,
tied in place by ropes
as thick as elephant legs.
I rub up against them,
watch you waver, then wince.
The path forward is no path.
Your pain of exile is the balm
of walking. These many
years of walking.

I Pour the Royal Wine

Root-like and gnarled, my hand slides across the
    desk, sidles
onto a blue-white tile from Delft. How cool the
    touch of porcelain.
I have shaped backsplashes of poems against
    the tides of time. Waves
surge across the wall, wash away spills of libations.
    I pour the royal wine,
let it drip between my fingers: a birthright's stain.
    I brush a rough cast
of my hand. Knotted bones creak. My shaky reach
    outlasts my grasp.

Until Only Colors Exist

the sycamore sheds
its rough gray skin
unveiling dead wood
as hard as oak
as pale as a bashful girl's eyes
look deep within them
to see the world afloat

born for another time
the tree shoots up
straight and tall
sprouting leaves and buds
beneath the hot spring sun
life ignores appearances
stirs silently below the belt
to breed each unwitting kind

I have held onto
the sycamore's
reptilian bark
I have unearthed
its roots as totems
of rebirth of newness
of life that encapsulates
us all engendering blind trust
in nature's driven ways

I am bound for another
country that waters
my desires for longevity
feeds my pangs for blossoming
under the aegis of the sun
until only colors exist
and I vanish beneath them
afloat in a barque
atop this ocean
of pale pastels

Wilderness

without compass or map
find the pace
that pricks your conscience
into thinking you've made
a pilgrim's progress
against the wind

count the bats as they flee
the mouths of caves
swirling clouds in flight
they lasso the fading light
tighten their grip on the night
dip and swoop
with delight
burrow toward
the break of day

nature flings its graces in our path
they glimmer like mica in uncut stones
we collect them
set pieces of the land
only to find they do not belong
among the living
only the dead can
grasp their shiny surfaces

tomorrow I will leave the desert
for the welcome mat of home
little will go with me little will remain
except the emptiness
of the seeking self
turning over each rock
to catch a lizard scurrying past

riches embedded in the mind
cannot be stolen only rearranged

I will take the adolescent bat
release him to the moon
then make my dwelling
in the first open cave

Love Never Dies

love never dies
its body is the Other
whom we can never reach
we cradle it in our mind
caress its imaginary flesh
then preserve it as *caritas*
fixing it forever
above the stars

love never dies
the beloved swirls around
the center of our wills
teasing out obedience
to her beauty
which washes over us
like a mountain stream
her voluptuous body
mesmerizes tempting
us with Eros
and promises
of endless joy

love never dies
it races like atrial fibrillation
across our hollow chests
soars over
every limit to desire
rips away each sluggish
shred of doubt
renews the quick
and the dead
traces a lineage
of ecstasy and longing
we will never shake off
its brilliance
and endless allure

A Question of Magnitude

suns circulate like dust motes in the air
they clash and angle off clouds
take aim and push the smallest orb
into the path of overheated meteors

where do we belong
alone on the edge of the moon
half-buried in darkness
half-formed to the shape of planets
we bounce among them
into the sun's vast orbit
and sweat and sweat
throwing our clothes
into the fire that never dies

we must drink from liquid suns
that spill across our paths
sucking us into their provenance
pooling at our feet
wrapping around our heads
how do we resist the lure
of the king who flows
rather than rules from his throne
we imbibe a piece of his power
we burn a few errant cells
sniffing the scorching aroma of death

it is a question of magnitude
can the king die in his boots
can he draw his sword
behead the imposter in his court
or trifle with the bungling spy
who keeps his notes stuffed

in his waistcoat rumpled and damp
not accessible to the outsider looking in

I push the sun off his throne
usurp the little power that is mine
rise from my half-darkness
into ivory moonlight no melody plays
save Chopin's "Funeral March"
the passing days keep time
like a rusting metronome

This Blue-Green Rock

I climb the golden chain
that holds the world in place
it stretches beyond me
an infinite umbilical cord

to bear my weight each link
strains against the next
the pressure of the cosmos
the burden of being

from this pinnacle I behold
the minute machinations
of other planets O how
they spin O how they fly

Atlas shrugs and the globe
lands in my lap squirming
like an infant impatient
to move to feed to thrive

I search for the red dot
that marks my spot
on Earth a cave buried
beneath the sea

waters wash over me
marooned on this blue-green rock
pushing ever upward to wrap
the golden chain around me

The Emptiness Within

the oracle has abandoned Delphi
her link to Apollo broken
by the overweening needs
of my vacant mind

1.
winded I climb the hill
to the ruins of the temple
sheep bells clink in the distance
the sun burns my back
like Atlas I carry
the weight of the world
on my shoulders

Socrates made this pilgrimage
nearly three millennia ago
troubled by what he heard
he heeded the oracle's command
know thyself
and paid the ultimate price

2.
in the shadow of the ruins
I spread my meager lunch
on the greening grass
winds whip the corners
of my covers I secure them
with the point of a knife

here high above Greece
bumping up against
the stratosphere of Socrates
I marvel at the miracle
of self-consciousness
and begin to doubt my senses

resting my head against
a white-washed boulder
I doze in the noonday sun
its warmth caresses me
pulls out of me all I know
all I am dreaming

on the temple's lintel I stand tall
and balance in the breeze
I await my epiphany
I hunger for the wisdom of the gadfly
of Athens but find only silent stones
recriminating my weakness

3.
somewhere a lamb bleats hungry
and tired seeking its mother's milk
I bark back in agony
over the vacancy of my quest
ten thousand steps
and still not a word to be heard

resigned I climb down
as long shadows paint the hill
I must rescind my certainty
to learn what it means
to live and think like a man

on the downward path
I meet my old self scrambling up
eager for a taste of wisdom
confident of his final victory
thinking himself
Socrates incarnate
staring vacantly ahead
knowing nothing at all

First Do No Harm

rainwater pools at the low point
of the yard overshadowed
by a towering pin oak
tallest tree in town
or so say the arborists
their intent is only to climb not cut
first do no harm

in the half-moon theater
at Epidaurus I stand on stage
and recite the opening lines
of *Oedipus Rex* my voice
reverberating with perfect pitch
reaching the farthest seats
like an oracle proclaiming my fate

I scramble up the oak
settle in the crook of a branch
reach for a perch as high
as Agamemnon's throne
I hear sheep bells clang
in the vale they soothe me
as I survey my ruined kingdom

at first I do no harm in my dreams
of Greece I reshape them to fit
my earthly needs they tumble down
hillsides into erstwhile quarries
I chisel my block of stone smooth its edges
in the distance my father approaches
O Oedipus above all do no harm

Gravity

laughing bands of birds
saturate the sky
with melodies
I cannot fathom

rosy-fingered dawn spills waves
of light across the altar
I prepare the year-old lamb

I am Abraham knife raised
all doubts assuaged
in these pink-rimmed eyes

Death lures me to follow him
down avenues of dreams
how much I have known

how much I have forgotten
his dark figure approaches
with my knife bloodied and dull

roses shed their petals
mingle with the moon
I will break the bonds of gravity
before the birdsong fades

I Am You You Are Me

we break bread slice the fist-sized wheel of cheese
anticipate the crisp taste of cooling wine
beyond the gateway boulders of Marble Canyon
we sweep clean a niche from sandy folds of stone

they tower over us upending our poise as creatures
made in the image of a mountain god high enough
to avoid the scorn of giants low enough
to shelter love in tremors of the earth
we recline in shadow / the sun peeks over rims
of stone that encircle us / in them we find freedom
of being / in them we savor a sense of fruition

our lips lock in an instinctive embrace / our bodies float
in union taking their cues from the seer
of the heart I feel yours beating against my chest
rhythm of life of death of the delicate dance
into the winnowing sky / its cirrus clouds brush
together our names I am you you are me
O how the illusory self dissipates on the wind

Life's Human Face, Human Grace

1.
I will not learn this lesson again
beyond the wall a world awaits unfinished
    its elements akimbo
like detritus from a storm
no plan shows how to build anew

my mind roams mired in night
in the mystery of dreams
vivid colors serpentine stories fear and panic
none coughs up a catharsis
none conjures a clue
    to the magic of the unconscious

2.
I have followed the Stations of the Cross
embraced their path of suffering
at the end a vision shows a citadel
on a hill of verdant pastures
I look again but do not see my face

I shape my world from sun blood and soil
imagine a life without them
and you have robbed it
of its human face its human grace
to shoulder the mortal burden
of this undiscovered country

Other Nutrients Nourish Me Now

horses saunter in the mist
palominos and frothy browns
they see past the pasture's edge
bound into the vast unknown

I lean on an agèd fence post
it bears my weight then wobbles
as the sun rises behind the hills
hoof prints spell *freedom*

high in the cottonwoods I gain
a God's-eye view of the horses
I would descend a *deus ex machina*
but they have no need to believe

wisps of cotton cling to my teeth
other nutrients nourish me now
beauty lays its bounty before me
I taste then race into the vast unknown

These Dark Shores

sea waves rise like dragons
descend as coffins of foam
they baptize me in sprays
of sea salt and brine

I am helpless against the tides
they surge across my feet
recede into the flood
reclaim these dark shores

a skiff tied to a shaky pier
bounces on the waves
it holds the lure of hope
the promise of escape

I retrace my steps in the sand
follow footprints of a ghost
against the sea wall I lean
waiting for darkness to lift

Ascent

my hand punctures a cloud
tickles the glimmer of stars
glitter dapples my thumb
burns like wildfire up my arm

how high we climb on the wings
of art how low we stoop
to scoop flecks of gold
our miner's pan swills with hope

somewhere in the Rocky Mountains
streams splash against stone
burrow through meadows wash
the sludge of life from a hiker's boots

I step past wildflowers pick the brightest
climb to the plateau of contemplation
one false move and all images collapse
I ride the cloud into burning light

The Book of Water

I drink from the book of water
its pages lap against my tongue
tepid tempests in a koi pond

I thirst for the elegance of the poem
where the protagonist is no-self
where the shore washes away desire

truth troubles us with its indifference
it seeks the absolute but drowns
in a relativity of worlds doused in doubt

I need not swim to find my way
I need not exhale what buoys me into the future
light wavers on the waves a reluctant beacon

when we last floated hand in hand
each stroke separated us below the surface
our poem dog-paddled into turgid depths

I would drink freely of you again but the pages form
no funnel they splash wetness to my taste
hold fast to my journey's aim not yet to die

Now We Rise Skyward

1.
the canyon floor
beckons like a siren
I plug my ears
claw the limestone walls
check my descent
as I fall ever earthward

no footsteps but mine
mold the sand
a sheet of glass
births diamonds
in the dying light
I overload my pack
with riches along
this pitted path

2.
purple swoops
saturate the clouds
the day's final tableau
of beneficent fire
I hear the ancient wash
of sighs bathe
the Western Wall
inwardly I wail
bang my head
against stone

I cast back to your
pirouette in the pines
your lithe body
called to me

a tone purer
than sirens

now we rise
skyward
to be reborn
in the eternal
kiss of the wind

TRACES OF THE HOLY: FOR THE DYING

"We part only to be
more intimately at one,
more divinely at peace with all,
with each other. We die so as to live."

—Friedrich Hölderlin

I Rise to the Sky

Older than the canyon walls,
the bristle-cone pine screws up
its courage to welcome the dawn.
Few signs of life shoot into the mist.
Few pieces of bark split beneath
the sky's bright ax. If trees could worship,
the pine would prostrate before the sun.
I trip along the canyon's lip.
Snow patches my path.
Bright colors buoy the azure dome.
A donkey brays as a pilgrim packs
his wares in the cave of the sun.
I clutch its ragged beams, bow to the pine.

Inferno

orange tiles undulate across rooftops
rainwater pools in alternating U's
stone faces stare down
at the glistening street
they neither frown nor grin
their gaze locked and loaded
on what outlasts the rain

this is the skeleton of Florence
an Italianate aura beams
from jigsaw lanes
roof tiles add color
to the kingdom of the mundane
I will step over them
in my journey to the sky

in the corner of my eye I spy
Dante larger than life
hawkish punitive
contemplating the depths
of degradation in the human soul
his vision lassoes me
into the first circle of Hell
there minimal tortures await
orange rooftops burst into flames

I Will Guard My Dreams

chainsaws moan as they slice
the midriff of the dying sycamore
exiled from the Earth it resists its unsightly end
rooted in place sap seeping it sheds its limbs
returning to its nascent state
of freshly planted seeds

lightning growls as it exits the tree
only a small black wound remains
unnoticed until the leprous bark sheds
its shades of gray and white
squirrels scurry at its base careening
off their vanishing playground

I groan as life completes
another turn around the sun
before grinding to an impasse
nature is its own nemesis
beauty ends in tawdry scenes of decay
death claims its own with a tired grin

the Earth weeps as the naked trunk
crashes to the ground the thud
shudders through my quiet bungalow
we now live in a desecrated neighborhood
no longer is the view framed by upright sentries
tonight I will guard my dreams
from the chainsaw's growl

We Eat; Therefore, We Are

1.
The nor'wester blows me back to the beginning of time.
Chronos devours his young, orally fixated on the mystery
of existence. We eat; therefore, we are. I lose my appetite
as wave after wave of a tsunami crashes at my feet.

This, the only mortal path across the tar-infected beach.
Travelers march on, consuming with their eyes
the riches of the Oregon coast. O how exquisite
is the beauty of a basalt-barricaded beach.

Where we turn for shelter, comfort, and home
is not signposted. We seek it out by instinct.
I see a starfish cling to a black boulder, its
pink flesh broiling in the afternoon sun.

How far must I travel to leave the murderous
business of time? In the foamy sand,
prints from noisy gulls spread
to the horizon. Between them, I breathe.

2.
If we cannot conceive it, does infinity exist?
My steps head southward to California
and Mexico, ancient cultures whose mores
could not be more different: geographic oxymorons.

Now is the time to declare all territory my own.
Consciousness intends only what makes it aware. It aims
its gaze at unseen essences, even though all around me
lies the physical. Elemental, burrowing into my gut.

I will trace the highways of the gods. Long dead, they
reappear to weigh down modern verse with a hint
of transcendence. Nothing else supplies us meaning.
Nothing else loves us as a crab does the sea.

The Burden of Nothingness

a smudge of white tattoos the azure sky
flattop mountains encircle our camp
I laze by the fire stare at the sun
bump your shoulder as you wake

a caravan creeps across the desert floor
green is not at home here only tans
and browns I brush the horizon
with blue then touch its vanishing point

I cannot recall when I first set foot
on this arid soil wild donkeys watched
as I stumbled past cacti and caches
of sand water eluded my every step

now the sky burns in a yellow haze
light settles on my next move I haul
the pack onto my back the burden of
nothingness drives me to my knees

the day settles into itself
fleet feet skim the paths
of heavily wooded hills
the goddess of belonging
grabs your hand pulls you
to safety then hurls you
into the heavens
each higher stratum
hardens like ice
rain freezes on your face

you have outstripped
the sun you have

surpassed your guide
reward her with
well-worn bags
of gold florins
we cannot escape the husk
of freedom in these
overweening years
to peel it back to nothing
requires a will free
of the petty conflicts
of egos
mine yours
each biting clawing
for blood each pinned
to the sorrowful Earth

let us weave blankets
of fresh pine needles
let us seal them in sap
and lie together as if
it were our last night
on Earth as if
we had no recourse
but to wait and die
settled as these hills

To Walk or Rest

we look back
along the road
to immortality
ravines and rivers
block our way
an ankle turns
a knee goes out
we smear balm
on aging bones
nightingales sing
the rains begin
one more step
and our goal recedes
to walk or rest
is all the same

I Widen the Map's X

I climb the rocky stairwell
one stagger at a time
and reach the summit
of my lookout
lined with planks
of knotted pine

here trees squirm
under gravity's thumb
I clear their canopy catch
a glimpse of new growth
sap rises in my eyes
seeps through my brain

drenched in the *élan vital*
I draw a map to the treasure
of our marriage unwilling
to settle for memory's bright mirage
tonight the moon will burnish
my dreams with beams of you

nothing keeps my spirit in place
like the march of mercury
first my neck and face broil
then embers smolder like lava
snug and warm I widen the map's X
singed by this flame of love

Every Angel Is Terror

Rilke paces past the parapets
of Duino Castle / thunder rattles
the black-slate roof / tiles tumble
into shattered rubble that blocks
the groundskeeper's path / he peers
into the black sky and trembles

Rilke obsesses on the host
of angels descending to Earth
lightning strikes a century-old pine
sparks and splinters sputter to the sea
only water can heal / only waves
can assuage the anguished self

Who, if I cried out, would hear me among the Angelic
Orders? And even if one were to suddenly
take me to its heart, I would vanish into its
stronger existence. For beauty is nothing but
the beginning of terror, that we are still able to bear,
and we revere it so, because it calmly disdains
to destroy us. Every Angel is terror.

terror trails Rilke to his chambers / cold gloomy
as welcoming as death / why must we torment
ourselves to produce great art to write the poem
that expresses all poetry that traps in its net
the ground and goal of Being / who breaks free
who hides behind bulkheads as rain pummels

I map the path Rilke takes toward dawn over Trieste
the lambent light woos the dreamer awake
sun crackles through clouds showers the earth
    with warmth

I sense the brush of angel wings / blood drains
    from my face /
have I seen a ghost / am I drunk on terror
    has Rilke sung
the final word of beauty that spurs us ever closer
    to our death

Desert Elegy

1.
angels pound the finishing stones in place
her grave burgeons with scarves and jewels
they cling to the casket like barnacles
they adhere to what kicks underground
sheep meander in search of clumps of green
angel tools predate the Earth / they wrestle the soil
consecrate their place in it Gaia gapes in astonishment
spirit and intellection sling the Big Bang
toward its birthing pangs / clouds assume
the forms of wings light irradiates itself
all shines white the eye's pure gold

2.
I trudge the salt beds of Death Valley
lowest place in the hemisphere
hottest place this side of Hell / you must make
the desert your lover / you must build
ephemeral altars out of emptiness and ocher
you must test the depths of graves
they shrink in the sun / donkeys keep watch over them
in pairs / they notice nuance / a tear signals malady
a sob the long-awaited deluge
I admire the colors of their coats and walk on

3.
in my dreams angels wear overcoats
and elongated faces like donkeys / they disapprove
of my waywardness and brush dirt from their hands
dust to dust one proclaims as the sun dies into night
only to rise again / its absence chills my bones
its presence scalds my scalp / I stumble upon the gray
wooden handle of a shovel laid parallel to her grave

Grass Dance

1.
Spirits trample the rain-starved
plains like herds of fattened buffalo.

Cloaked in tawny hides, they pound
the earth: invincible grass dancers.

From the ground spring their harvests
of sickness and health, good and evil.

A shaman ignites his sage bundle,
tosses pebbles on the tipi floor.

He stumbles backward, eyes turned
inward, arms outstretched to receive

the medicine's blessing. He soars in vapor
trails of hawks, surpassing the smoke,

the sky, the spirits' singing to the drum
beat, the cosmos' luminous fringe.

Eyes on fire like liquid lightning,
he peers into the future, the past,

liberates forces of healing, gathers up
baskets of goodness, effusive with wonder.

2.
Above the dusty brown hills, the turquoise
sky casts shadows on ancestral shores.

All must cross the waters, awaken from
their trances, devour supernatural dreams.

The shaman cries out in ancient rapture,
his flesh on tenterhooks, shredding into leaves

of supplication, tears of blood and water.
Horses snort in the distance. Raptors

circle overhead. The shaman grapples
with the spirits, sucks power from their

dances, grinds grasses' green seedlings,
the growing treasure of the earth.

This Shadowland

death is a mystery
and a sorrow
Juliet lays her head
on Romeo's cold chest
plunges a dagger
in her heart
at last they unite in love

we make our path
through this shadowland
a rocky trail between canyon walls
no signage no maps
is this the shining next turn
is this the road of no passage
we see through a glass darkly

and now the day flicks
its hazy eyelids shut
in a dreamless sleep
here all ways lie open
we will fly above them
into the dense woods
beyond the blue horizon

blood on the flagstones
will not wash away
the dagger clatters
to an ignoble ending
death solves nothing
its rotten finger buried
in the hollow of our heart

Ghosts

ghosts no longer haunt me
in this thin state of confusion
I see gray where they see nothing
force of habit drives them from their perch
ever deeper into the Earth's fiery core
where they claim to cherish the flames

I shun all contact with them now
I write from the well of my imagination
ignore their nudges to notice
the dull details of their reality
proud like chest-thumping apes
they flash their yellow fangs and roar

I cannot conjure belief in them anymore
though they insist on oppression and grief
though they reek of brimstone and sweat
their slim slip of power mimics the tawdry
crown of a self-appointed tyrant

ghosts no longer lurk on limbs in shadow
at dawn their habitat will be clear-cut
lumps of ugly soil laced with fragments of bark
nowhere have they left a lasting mark
tonight they will return to rebut my litany
    of rejections

Immortality

The wren dies on the branch,
old age toppling into dust.
Its mate squawks in the top
of the canopy, confused
at the sudden stillness, lost
without an echoing song.

I watch it rustle the leaves,
flit back and forth along limbs,
frantic to revive its love, frowning
at its newfound loneliness, gasping
for a communal air to breathe. I have
been this bird, wrapped in blue sorrows,

mindless in grief, saving my
tears for the coming drought,
hoping that immortality is more
than longevity. Do I not cater
to suffering, fill up vessels
of loss with these dusty elegies?

Tonight I will bury the old wren
in catacombs of leaves. I will
wash down the walls, lay fresh
sprigs of thyme, buy another few
seconds to mourn its mate's
unknowing grief: *Only pain is immortal.*

Satisfaction

I was born on a moonlit bridge
as the river surged. My name
not yet announced, my fate
not yet fixed. When my mother
took her last step onto dry land,
she jostled me and I whimpered.
From that day forward I have failed
to wail. Another slap on my
bottom makes no difference.
I cannot give satisfaction.

As I grew, deer skittered past.
They seemed so frail, nervous,
flitting, skimming fences, running
for their lives. My uncle took me
hunting once when I was older.
I was sickened at the sight of blood.
Even then I did not weep, but
plotted my revenge. Tempting
death proved to be as tedious
as singing the praises of venison.

In the last year of school, before
the war, I stopped eating meat.
Grinding flesh and veins seemed
as barbaric as the way animals
were killed, a hammer to the head,
and the angus buckles to the ground.
Nietzsche and Dostoevsky predicted
our nihilistic inheritance: If God is dead,
everything is permitted. Worse, it is we
who have killed Him. He will not give satisfaction.

A Good Soldier at His Post

I stand beside the bed
my grandmother died in.
She lies smothered
in blankets, her bleary eyes
focused on Heaven,
her mind preoccupied
with counting her children,
anointing them to carry on
her mission of love in the world.

My body aches with the restless
cares of my age. Standing still,
anxious and squirming, unsure
of where her next breath might come,
I gasp when I hear what
I imagine to be her death rattle.
It is only an instinctive wheeze
eating air as lemon cake *à la mode*.

Birds keep their peace. Is it the heat?
The waterfall of light? I no longer
calculate answers to these riddles.
I no longer care about being right.
It is enough to stand and wait,
a good soldier at his post. I touch
her hand, it weakly responds.
The pulse flinches. Her breathing sours.

When she passes, I am there,
hewed to my post, fast asleep.

The Pose of the Dead

I don the mask of Don Giovanni
unfurl my cape in the morning breeze
await my horses to prance through woods
pose as the prince of this world supreme

the path of Eros is filled with pitfalls
I have dragged myself out of them
major impulses minor desires all risks
to become the Other behind this mask

whose face beams so secluded
whose voice filters through
this exquisite design when
I flee myself I am most alive

now a cuckold gallops behind me
an old man I cannot outrun
he cries *pistols at dawn* soon
I shall assume the pose of the dead

Six-Beat Bars

sestina glides down
my spine lodging
in a lockbox
of word and spirit
each movement
stands for itself
and something else
each metaphor
makes my face
into its own
nowhere does
the heartbreak
of dying sting
so deeply
as in the languor
of lost love

I take up my pen
to impale the ghost
of passion it haunts
my storytelling stuck
in a skein of yarn
then stitched
into a cape
that cushions
my wounds and scars
that scatters my mind
into myriad bits
of stanzas and lines
nowhere does
the loss of sense
wrap around
my throat
with such
murderous intent

at night I feel
myself falling
from a vertigo
of being
one step into
the abyss and
anxiety becomes
my new mantle
choose only
the self you would
become kiss goodbye
only the lover
of your mind
fade only
in six-beat bars
counting them
as they slide into
staccato heartbeats

A Coat of Molten Bark

Between the lines of chicken scratching, I search
    for traces of thoughts past.
Who I was when this journal began, I am no longer.
    A stranger to myself.
Yet something endures, a continuum of selves,
    episodic and strong.
Lightning flashes over my home, a frisson
    of illumination in the night.
So many trees have died, nature's assassinations,
    denouements of smoke.
Now I read my first will and testament, a coat
    of molten bark, rings of fire.

And So Nature Glides By

The fat spruce swoons, frozen above ground.
Branches taut, tethered in snow. Wind moans
as it shuffles the tiniest birds south. No warmth
at hand. No ghostly heatwaves shimmy

above the road. And so Nature glides by,
a ubiquitous stranger, never settled
in our town, never fixed. I would ride
this gale to its origins, but guards repel

the curious. These secrets belong only to those
who stamp the eye of God on ice-laden soil.
Winter drains our blood, leaves its red monogram
on pristine fields of white. Tracks of bobcats fade.

I cling to divots where foliage blooms. Refugees
of green poke their heads through a crusty brown
veil. Beneath it, another world spins, as cold
as Dante's Hell, as hard as the bitter stones of snow.

Epicurean Delights

1.
A sky of wonders opens its arms
to the rose-dappled dawn. Light refracts
through my one good eye. I see nothing
but cirrus streaks of lavender and pink.

Let me paint them after I secure
a canvas, brushes, and tubes of cyan.
My world lies tangled up in blue.

2.
Days pass like pebbles in a mountain stream.
We carry the virus of time in our bellies. It lives
within, saturates what remains, then brands
our backs with its contorted signs.

At last, I shall not be rustled. My will
already broken, my mind liberated
from the cycles of love and death.

3.
I tear off a piece of this artisan bread. Crumbs
form a cairn. I would stand by it but I am Cyclops,
peering into the future, with sirens wailing at my back.
I will build a strait and narrow highway, then walk it
alone.

4.
A crescendo of freedom raises the hair on my neck.
A frisson of caution slaps my hands. What I hold
dear is buried in the dawn. It captivated Homer, who
clamped down on broadswords each time he wrote.

5.
I am no longer mesmerized by light. Sun and shadow
mate like a bull in a lowing herd. He lays his full weight
on the cows' broad backs. They withstand his wild-eyed
frenzy. His Epicurean delights nourish the earth.

The Water Turned Hope

angel wings flutter
from a mackerel sky
they hover above us
buoyant on the wind

I have been looking up
so long I no longer see
the Earth below me
all is but an azure wash

I stagger to the edge
of a jagged crevasse
one slip and I will fall
and fight then rise alone

walking never ends
it makes my path
lets sunlight fade
into the wondrous dark

I shall not fly again
among feral clouds
they unfurl a canopy
of waters to imbibe

my hands work as well
as a chalice I will sip
the water turned hope
nestled among
these tarnished wings

Death Mask

1.
Let the plaster
settle, still malleable
enough to lift off
cheekbones and lips,
still moist enough
to peel back
in one piece,
your physiognomy
intact, your character
caressed
into every crevice
or wrinkle
or hand-smoothed
plane of flawless
skin. O how
the living must
envy you.

2.
Pascal's nose:
long, narrow
slightly flared,
as if forever
sniffing
at the world,
disabused of the glory
that birthed his misery.
Just try it: Place yourself
in an empty room
with utterly nothing
to do. Boredom kills.
It begets madness.

It begets despair.
It teeters behind
absurdity, riding the fence:
Another mask, another life?

3.
Death mask, life mask.
There is no difference
in vitality, both staid
from materials that
freeze the features,
fixed, no longer viable.
Watch how they
harden into rigid forms
of wounded love.
Timeless, all art
piggybacks on a pulse
not its own. All life
bathes in time as a sow
frolics in pools of mud:
Self-consciousness melts
into waves and waves of pleasure.
Plaster chips: time's envy.

ABOUT THE AUTHOR

Arlice W. Davenport is the author of five full-length books of poetry and three chapbooks. All have been published by Meadowlark Press or Meadowlark Poetry Press in Emporia, Kansas.

His academic background includes degrees in philosophy, literature, French, and religious studies, along with a concentration of work in art history.

He and Norman Carr—whose abstract paintings have adorned the covers of Davenport's most recent books—have been friends for more than 40 years, traveling together internationally, along with Davenport's wife, Laura. He lives in Wichita, Kansas.

Davenport participates in the 2024 Local Authors Day at the Wichita Public Library.

ACKNOWLEDGMENTS

Making a book is a lot like a battle: You can't reach your goal without enlisting the right help. Fortunately, for this fifth book published by Meadowlark Press, I enlisted the best help out there.

Tracy Million Simmons—as publisher of Meadowlark Press, she effortlessly guides her ships into harbor. Somewhere, she has a magic switch that turns the daunting into the comfortable. I lay my many thanks at her feet.

As the head of Meadowlark Poetry Press, **Linzi Garcia** has once again used her subtleties, poetic acumen, and sensitivity to the direction my book is taking, to make meaningful changes and improvements to my manuscript. She is relentless in her editing. And having her at the helm is a great assurance for me. As always, she can be counted on for top-flight work. (Please ignore any mixed metaphors in what I've written here.)

Norman Carr, a nonobjective painter in Wichita, Kansas, has contributed his paintings to my last three books and one chapbook. If you are interested in learning more about the *Traces of the Holy* painting, please see my essay, "The Unifying Force of Nonobjective Painting," at ncarrstudio.com, under the Journal heading.

I also want to thank **Natalie Wolf**, an intern at Meadowlark, who pitched in on copy editing and many other helpful projects. I benefitted from her learning on the job.

Finally, I would be aimlessly wandering in circles without the support of my wife, **Laura**. She stands by me on some of my long nights/early mornings as I wrestle like Jacob with the angel. Jacob wound up with an injured hip; all I have to show is an itchy trigger finger, which spends its time hitting "Send."

NOTES

"Hymn for Hölderlin"
Fredrich Hölderlin was a German Romantic poet of the eighteenth and nineteenth centuries. He wrote, among other themes, of the twilight of the classical Greek gods. The philosopher Nietzsche picked up on this idea, applying it to Christianity, in his book *Twilight of the Idols*. The portrait of Hölderlin was painted by Franz Carl Hiemer. The painting is public domain and was retrieved from *Poetry Foundation*'s website.

"Descartes Redux"
René Descartes is a seventeenth-century French philosopher who made famous the phrase, "Cogito, ergo sum," which translates to, "I think, therefore I am."

"First Do No Harm"
Epidaurus was an ancient Greek city known as a center of miraculous healing. Its theater, built in the fourth century B.C., was considered the most perfect in Greece for acoustics and aesthetics. Oedipus is a prominent figure in Greek mythology. He unwittingly killed his father and married his mother. When he learned this, he put out both his eyes. Agamemnon was the king of Mycenae, Greece, and figured prominently in Homer's *Iliad* and other ancient Greek literary works.

"Every Angel Is Terror"
The featured excerpt is from Rainer Maria Rilke's poem, "First Duino Elegy," translated by J. B. Leishman and Stephen Spender in *Duino Elegies* (Hogarth Press, 1939).

Books are a way to explore, connect, and discover. Poetry invites us to observe and think in new ways, bridging our understanding of the world with our artistic need to interact with, shape, and share it with others.

Publishing poetry is our way of saying:
We love these words,
we want to preserve them,
we want to play a role in sharing them
with the world.

Follow Meadowlark Press
on Facebook & Instagram

ⓕ facebook.com/ReadAMeadowlarkBook

◉ @meadowlarkbooks

www.ingramcontent.com/pod-product-compliance
Lightning Source LLC
Chambersburg PA
CBHW071608170426
43196CB00034B/2218